Franklin Vinícius M. Dutra

Affirmative Action in Brazilian Higher Public Education and John Rawls

Franklin Vinícius M. Dutra

Affirmative Action in Brazilian Higher Public Education and John Rawls

ScienciaScripts

Imprint
Any brand names and product names mentioned in this book are subject to trademark, brand or patent protection and are trademarks or registered trademarks of their respective holders. The use of brand names, product names, common names, trade names, product descriptions etc. even without a particular marking in this work is in no way to be construed to mean that such names may be regarded as unrestricted in respect of trademark and brand protection legislation and could thus be used by anyone.

Cover image: www.ingimage.com

This book is a translation from the original published under ISBN 978-620-2-04098-3.

Publisher:
Sciencia Scripts
is a trademark of
Dodo Books Indian Ocean Ltd. and OmniScriptum S.R.L publishing group

120 High Road, East Finchley, London, N2 9ED, United Kingdom
Str. Armeneasca 28/1, office 1, Chisinau MD-2012, Republic of Moldova, Europe
Managing Directors: Ieva Konstantinova, Victoria Ursu
info@omniscriptum.com

Printed at: see last page
ISBN: 978-620-8-41294-4

To Anilde, Francielle and Ana, with all my love.

ACKNOWLEDGMENTS

I would like to thank all those who contributed to my education, the great teachers I had from a very young age, in the person of Profs. Drs. Thomas da Rosa de Bustamante and Leandro Martins Zanitelli. I must also mention my home, the Federal University of Minas Gerais, for the incredible opportunity to study law there. My thanks to the National Council for Scientific and Technological Development for funding me with a scientific initiation scholarship. My dear friends, Rodolfo, Arthur, Hesick, Rafael, Daniel, Stephanie, Naiana, Magno, Andre, Yago, Robson, Henrique, Vinicius, Deivide, Igor, Mirlir, and so many others are never forgotten. None of this would have been possible without the support of my family, Pedro, Margarida, Anilde, Nivaldo, Francielle, Anilson, Fabiana, Pedro (Spider-Man), Catarina, Aunt Kennya, Valter and Priscila, thank you very much! Thank you to my love, Ana, for always being by my side. In short, thank you to everyone I've mentioned and to the countless others whom I've wronged by not naming here!

Imagination is more important than knowledge.

Albert Einstein

We are all equal before moral duty.

Immanuel Kant

SUMMARY

This paper seeks to clarify the relationship between the philosophy of John Rawls and affirmative support for access to public higher education institutions. In this way, the question is whether or not Justice as Fairness legitimizes the policy of educational quotas.

To this end, its main theoretical points are outlined and the concept of affirmative action adopted is presented and related. The initial understanding of Justice as Fairness is fundamental to understanding the rest of the presentation.

The argument is made to distinguish each of the layers of affirmative support presented, combining them with both ideal and non-ideal theory. From this contrast, we find the conditions and philosophical justification for certain levels of affirmative support.

Finally, having clarified the categories of affirmative support that Egalitarian Liberalism considers to be morally justifiable, a brief comment is made on Brazilian social quotas. For this, the parameters are those of Law No. 12.711/2012, which provides for quotas in the context of admission to universities and federal institutions of technical education at the secondary level.

Keywords: Political philosophy. Law. John Rawls. Affirmative support.

INDICE

Chapter 1 6

Chapter 2 10

Chapter 3 19

Chapter 4 36

Chapter 5 42

Chapter 6 45

1. METHODOLOGICAL INTRODUCTION.

Affirmative action policies have been much discussed in Brazil recently. This debate has even led to the drafting of a law specifically to deal with the issue in the context of access to public higher and technical education, Law No. 12.711/2012.

On the other hand, there still seems to be plenty of room for discussion about the moral legitimacy of the issue. Of course, this paper does not attempt to find the final solution to the case of affirmative action as a public policy in general. Nor does it hope to find the definitive solution to the problem within Rawlsean theory, since it is a matter of debate among its interpreters.

The objectives here are much more specific. It questions the philosophical justification for the existence of such policies on access to public higher education institutions, using the thought of John Rawls as a theoretical framework. This author was adopted because of his great influence on Western political philosophy since the second half of the 20th century and the strength of his arguments.

In this sense, the aim is to clarify a possible philosophical justification for affirmative action, or at least which affirmative action the theory can justify. In short, the question of this work is whether Justice as Fairness provides elements to support affirmative support, both racial and social, for admission to public higher education institutions, especially federal universities.

The exposition of the text begins with very general and introductory notes and clarifications about John Rawls' theory. The purpose here is simply to outline the general lines of this way of thinking, which permeates the basic discussion of the work. The theory's principles of justice are therefore outlined, explained and some observations and comments made by the author's readers on the topics dealt with.

The arguments for justifying the principles of justice in Rawls' theory are also examined. The most famous of these is the hypothetical social contract: the original position in which individuals are clothed in the veil of ignorance. It is believed that, in some way, the aspects of the theory initially explained are relevant to the question we are trying to answer here.

This is followed by a step into both Justice as Fairness and affirmative support itself. The next chapter, taking Robert Taylor's discussion as a basis, brings a stratified concept of affirmative support and applies it to two different nuances of Justice as Fairness, the ideal and the non-ideal theory.

The concept of affirmative action is divided into five different categories. It is worth noting that, in practice, public policies can fall into more than one category at the same time. In fact, this is believed to be the rule rather than the exception. Consequently, this division is for didactic and methodological purposes only.

Now that we have delimited the concept of each of the categories of affirmative support, the reflection turns to which of them is justifiable or even reconcilable with John Rawls' theory. However, for this, a theoretical conceptual division will play a key role: the distinction between ideal and non-ideal theory.

To understand this distinction, two ideas must be kept in mind. The first relates to the conditions, i.e. the social context in which each of these theories is inserted and the way in which society deals with the principles of justice and discrimination. The second, more intrinsically linked to the principles of justice themselves, differentiates each of the theories by the way in which the hierarchy between the principles is conceived. In the process, some comments are made on the relationship between these concepts and the Brazilian reality.

Having outlined the general panorama of Rawls' theory and materialized the concept of affirmative action applied to it, there is still one question left for the next chapter to tackle. In Brazil, it seems that the most necessary quota policy is the social one. Bearing in mind the entire context of Brazilian society, leaving aside any regional nuances, the mismatch that is usually seen between public and private primary education is one of the factors that most distorts access to university (and even the competition for jobs and social positions).

Not to mention, of course, the obvious disadvantages that the lower-income population has compared to the wealthier ones when it comes to the various paid extracurricular activities. These forms of supplementary education, such as tutoring, language classes and so on, are yet another way of widening the gap between competitors, making the outcome of the competition very doubtful. In this sense, it is understood that this is the point most in need of some kind of corrective public action.

In this context, it can be seen that a policy of social quotas, aimed at reducing morally arbitrary differences, is at the heart of the American theory, so that they are not just acceptable, but demands of justice. In this sense, they derive from the very principle of equal opportunities.

There are various instruments through which this type of policy can be implemented. The point is that, as outlined in the second chapter, we adopt the position that Justice as Fairness is uncomfortable with quotas for raising grades or reserving places. However, this position only exists under certain conditions. It is sad to say that Brazil has not even glimpsed the non-ideal conditions and is still a long way from them. This could mean, however, that because it is not in a situation where quotas affect equal opportunities, it is a policy that should be taken into account, given the Brazilian reality.

Given the country's profound social and economic inequalities , there does seem to be a place for "light" and "heavy" quotas. In order to reconcile this idea with the one presented in the previous chapters, the idea is that quotas should be used as a palliative, with the aim of seeking non-ideal conditions when they will no longer be necessary.

In this sense, they must be treated instrumentally and temporarily, just as affirmative action is acceptable under non-ideal conditions, but not accepted under ideal conditions. In other words, given the requirements of respect for the essence of the theory, good instrumentality and temporality, there seems to be nothing to prevent the presence of social quotas (and even combined, in some way, with racial quotas, given that racial prejudice is still systematically impregnated in Brazilian society).

In short, therefore, the hypothesis of the egalitarian legitimization of more aggressive affirmative action as a palliative in a society marked by the injustice of its institutions is reaffirmed. It is worth remembering, as a mere addendum, that for Rawls, it is not that those with natural gifts and better social conditions cannot benefit from them, but rather that inequalities will only be allowed if they improve everyone's situation (general conception of justice).

Finally, we conclude by revisiting the main themes covered in the chapters as described above and by addressing the central ideas and collecting the conclusions to which the argument has led. This brings the work to a close, in the hope of having provided a plausible and convincing explanation of this topic, which is so sensitive to Brazilian society today.

2. GENERAL NOTIONS OF JUSTICE AS EQUITY.

By way of introduction, it seems interesting to give a brief outline of the theory of justice we are dealing with in this work. It's worth pointing out at the outset that Rawls' major project in his book was to create a system of protection for certain rights regardless of the increase in overall benefit[1] . In other words, it is true that he wanted to find a viable alternative to Utilitarianism, a line of philosophy that has been a vast majority in the Anglo-American environment since its classic formulation with Jeremy Bentham and John Stuart Mill.

Of course, Utilitarianism and its more sophisticated versions still have considerable influence in the political philosophical debate, with exponents such as Peter Singer on its list of defenders. On the other hand, it is not disputed that the impact of John Rawls' work has been such that, in fact, the principle of utility has, to a certain extent, lost strength in the face of the Kantian alternative that has appeared.

There is also no doubt that the definitive answer as to whether Rawls or the utilitarians are right has not been found and probably will not be found, but that is no reason to end the debate. To avoid endless polemics, the text is limited to saying that at least certain forms of Utilitarianism taken to their ultimate consequences lead to results that greatly contradict our basic intuitions of justice .[2]

On the other hand, it should be noted that the idea of maximizing the happiness of the greatest possible number of people is very seductive and, at first, seems to have no flaws. Rawls himself seems to be trying to salvage what he can from Utilitarianism, especially with regard to efficiency in the

---

[1] KYMLICKA, Will. Contemporary Political Philosophy: An Introduction. 2°Ed. Oxford University Press. NY. 2002. P. 53.
[2] SANDEL, Michel J. Justipa: what is doing the right thing. Civilizapao Brasileira. Rio de Janeiro. 2015. PP. 30-39.

allocation of goods and social positions. However, it is not the purpose of this text to give an account of the debate between these philosophical currents: the aim of this introduction is merely historical contextualization.

To give a little more detail, it should be noted that, due to the very hegemony that Utilitarianism exercised, the only counterpoint was a set of ways of thinking called Intuitionism[3] . This did not, however, become a line of political philosophy *per se,* but something closer to a notion or sense of justice. This conception, although quite diverse in its subdivisions, is generally characterized by having a plurality of principles of justice, which lack a proper method and much less systematization.

For a reasonable period of time, therefore, this was Utilitarianism's interlocutor and it's no surprise why it remained almost hegemonic. To be fair, however, it may be that Intuitionism presents the most correct conception of justice and Rawls himself has a certain attraction to it[4] . However, since it is not a philosophical theory in the strict sense, given its lack of method, it is difficult to construct an argument on intuitionist grounds.

It was in this environment that Rawls launched his "Theory of Justice", rekindling the debate in political philosophy. Its first edition was published in 1971, although its primary ideas had already been conveyed in the academic environment in sparse texts and in various lectures given by the author since the previous decade. As already mentioned, Rawls seems to want to take advantage of some of the points he considers positive in Utilitarianism. However, given his Kantian roots, he has clearly shown himself to be one of the objectors of utility, perhaps the greatest of them in contemporary times.

In this way, his main objective was to develop a theory that would generate a political system whose structures were in line with our basic

[3] RAWLS, John. A Theory of Justice. Martins Fontes. Sao Paulo, SP. 2008. P. 41-49.
[4] RAWLS, John. A Theory of Justice. Martins Fontes. Sao Paulo, SP. 2008. P. 63.

intuitions of justice. In other words, he sought a theory whose conceptions, even when taken to their most far-reaching consequences, were not contrary to our sense of justice.

To do this, Rawls starts from a central idea (his general conception of justice) which, in fact, seems to be a good guide for interpreting his entire theory. In the author's own words :[5]

"(...) all primary social goods - freedom and opportunity; income and wealth; and the foundations of self-respect - should be equally distributed, unless an unequal distribution of any of them is to everyone's advantage."

With the above idea in mind, it is worth clarifying the Lexical System of Priorities[6] of his theory. Initially, it sounds somewhat unexpected to hear the word "lexical" in a theory of political philosophy: if this were a linguistic or philological tract, the strangeness would disappear. In Portuguese, lexico, in the broad sense, is almost synonymous with vocabulario. Daring a little in the assertions of this work, it seems that the author uses the term lexical to demonstrate the strength of his considerations, that is, the priority almost integrates the meaning, the concept of such principles.

That said, Rawls uses the Lexical System of Priorities to present the hierarchy between the principles of justice in his theory[7] . As a good liberal, the first principle is that of equal liberty. This means that the basic freedoms encompassed by the first principle can only be restricted if they increase general freedom. Therefore, freedom cannot be restricted in favor of the principle of difference.

---

[5] RAWLS, John. A theory of justice. 2nd Ed. Harvard University Press. Cambridge, MA. 1999. P. 54. Live translation.

[6] KYMLICKA, Will. Contemporary Political Philosophy: An Introduction. 2°Ed. Oxford University Press. NY. 2002. Pp. 55-57.

[7] RAWLS, John. A Theory of Justice. Martins Fontes. Sao Paulo, SP. 2008. P. 73.

The second principle is more problematic than the first, as it deals with social inequalities. The latter is divided into two nuances: inequalities should be allowed if they benefit the least advantaged and if they result from a fair distribution of opportunities between those who compete for social goods and positions.

Rawls did not give up having two principles, but, to be more precise, they are three. The second principle contains two principles which are in lexical order[8] . Thus, the second principle, for an influential part of the author's readers, is actually two: the principle of equal opportunities and the principle of difference .[9]

Equal opportunity (or fair equality of opportunity) prescribes that jobs and positions are open to those who seek them without unlawful distinctions. It is with this argument that Rawls combats morally arbitrary inequalities. With this principle, then, a cleaner competition is sought, one that makes jobs and positions available for open competition, with fair equality between competitors in mind. In this way, natural talents (natural determinisms) and social position (and other social determinisms) are prevented from influencing the outcome of the distribution of goods and social positions.

The principle of difference, on the other hand, aims to ensure that people only have the right to a greater share of social resources if they can demonstrate that this benefits everyone, including those with the smallest shares. It's as if Rawls had given the least advantaged in society a power of veto over inequalities, in a metaphor created by the author himself.

In fact, for Rawls, one of the assumptions that makes inequalities possible in society is that they are not the result of morally arbitrary motives,

[8] RAWLS, John. A Theory of Justice. Martins Fontes. Sao Paulo, SP. 2008. P. 376.

[9] BARRY, Brian. The Liberal Theory of Justice: A Critical Examination of the Principal Doctrines in A Theory of Justice by John Rawls. Oxford University Press. London, UK. 1973. Pp. 43-52.

but of the merit of each individual. By imposing a clear limit on the maximization of utility within his theory, the author clearly states that, even if the result of applying the principle of difference reduces society's utility, it will not be sacrificed. This protects certain fundamental individual rights, which will under no circumstances be suppressed. This idea is also underpinned by the very concept of existential minimum, which is the essence of the 1988 Constitution and is always raised in Brazilian case law.

In this logic, the aim was to create a system in which an individual's success or failure will be the result of the choices they make, in a context that allows for equal opportunities. Equal opportunities will be explained in more detail below. For now, the focus is on the idea of excluding morally arbitrary motives for determining the appropriate distribution of goods and social positions .[10]

These morally arbitrary determinisms fall into a first category, which encompasses those of economic and social origin, for example, being born into a wealthy family, resulting in access to a good education system which enables better job opportunities and, therefore, better pay. But Rawls goes further, also including natural determinism in his theory, i.e. natural gifts, such as having a high IQ or the innate creativity to compose symphonies.

The author's idea, in a nutshell, is to organize a structure in which these talents work to their maximum efficiency, until such time as allowing increased efficiency no longer creates advantages for those whose "fate" was not so friendly. In this system, no one deserves (or has an innate right to) the full benefits resulting from their natural gifts or the social position into which they were born. However, it is understood that it is not unjust to allow those who possess them to use them and obtain social benefits for themselves, as long as they work to improve the situation of those who were born into inferior

---

[10] KYMLICKA, Will. Contemporary Political Philosophy: An Introduction. 2°Ed. Oxford University Press. NY. 2002. Pp. 58-59.

social positions or were little favored by the chance of the natural lottery .[11]

Rawls then presents two arguments to support the fundamental principles of his theory. The first is that they are in line with our intuitions of justice, and the second is the argument of the social contract. Rawls himself recognizes that his first argument is not very strong, which is why he goes through it more succinctly. In fact, Rawls clearly prefers the social contract argument, which has become quite famous ("original position" is one of the best-known expressions of his theory). However, it is worth mentioning Will Kymlicka's position[12] , according to which, in fact, it is precisely because they are intuitive that the principles of justice are so strong. For this author, the second argument would be weaker, because Rawls designs his hypothetical contract so that it results in his principles of justice, so that if the argument of the social contract does not result in the two principles, Rawls expressly assumes that he would change its format so that this "error" could be corrected.

On this subject, he limits himself to saying that it seems that any corrections that might have to be made by the author to circumvent criticism would not reach the "heart" of the contract argument and would therefore not be fatal. As this is not the subject of this study, we will not delve into this discussion .[13]

In short, by saying that his principles of justice are intuitive, the author is saying that we can easily accept them, in other words, they go against the basic intuitions of human justice. It's an idea that sounds good, that

[11] KYMLICKA, Will. Contemporary Political Philosophy: An Introduction. 2°Ed. Oxford University Press. NY. 2002. P. 59.

[12] KYMLICKA, Will. Contemporary Political Philosophy: An Introduction. 2°Ed. Oxford University Press. NY. 2002. Pp. 60-61.

[13] Apologies to the reader if too much is made of this kind of statement, in other words, if a series of themes are touched on superficially and then abandoned. The pressing inexperience of the author, combined with a reasonable amount of reading of the great John Rawls, who has no qualms about doing this, are the reasons. Of course, the North American has the philosophical license to do so, which those of us who write here do not.

is, that the income and social position that each person occupies derive from real merit and not from factors that they haven't worked for (or aren't even in a position to have worked for).

Finally, we come to Rawls' social contract[14] . The first thing that needs to be clarified is that this argument is not intended to provide an explanation of what the transition from the "state of nature" to the "social state" would have been like, challenging the most accurate anthropology and proposing a historical fact, verifiable at some point during human evolution. In fact, the social contract is, in this conception, absolutely hypothetical. In the author's famous expression, it is not what we have done, but what we have done in a given situation.

In this way, he draws the original position, whose individuals must fulfill a series of requirements that, in short, mean a reduction in the personal information that each one has at their disposal. However, there are also other requirements, such as risk aversion, all of which converge in the sense of not allowing individuals to know in the slightest what position they will occupy in society, let alone what their natural gifts are. Rawls places the veil of ignorance over everyone's view of their original position .[15]

The purpose of this veil is to get individuals to discuss the principles of justice that will found that society, not with their personal position in mind, but with what would be best for the collective in mind. The purpose of resorting to the original position, as Rawls puts it, is "to exclude the principles that it would be rational for someone to propose for acceptance, however small the probability of success, if that person knew certain factors that, from the point of view of justice, are irrelevant."[16] In the original position, we have no idea what talents each person will have, what their social status will be, the

---

[14] KYMLICKA, Will. Contemporary Political Philosophy: An Introduction. 2°Ed. Oxford University Press. NY. 2002. Pp. 60-67.
[15] RAWLS, John. A Theory of Justice. Martins Fontes. Sao Paulo, SP. 2008. Pp. 165-173.
[16] Idem, p. 22.

benefits they will inherit, the level of ownership, in short, both natural and social contingencies that can determine the goods and social positions of individuals. It seems that the author's concern here is to create a scenario in which selfish motives do not interfere with the choice of the principles of justice: everyone reasons only on the basis of justice, with a view to creating a society that is as rationally just as possible.

The author also claims that every moral theory seeks to contemplate a project of what is considered a good life. In the case of his theory, a project for a good life can only be realized with a fair distribution of primary goods[17] : social (those distributed directly by social institutions) and natural (talents, which are affected by social institutions, but not directly distributed by them). Well, in the original position, everyone is looking for the form of distribution of primary goods that is best for everyone.

It is at this point that he makes use of another well-known argumentative resource in order to better explain the form of decision in the original post: the maximin strategy[18] (which is a
unfolding of the principle of difference). It is basically a way of escaping the risks of being in the worst position in a utilitarian (or libertarian) society, again to reinforce the argument that those in the original position would adopt his theory.

Well then, maximin, for Rawls, is the form of reasoning in his hypothetical contract according to which one seeks to maximize the social goods of those in the worst social position. On the other hand, then, according to the maximin, it is rational to choose the principles that lead to a social arrangement that provides those who are left with the least amount of primary goods with the maximum amount of them, given the various possible social

---

[17] KYMLICKA, Will. Contemporary Political Philosophy: An Introduction. 2°Ed. Oxford University Press. NY. 2002. Pp. 64-65.
[18] KYMLICKA, Will. Contemporary Political Philosophy: An Introduction. 2°Ed. Oxford University Press. NY. 2002. Pp. 66.

arrangements resulting from the principles of justice to be agreed upon.

In view of the above, the author believes that this mental exercise results in his two principles of justice. In other words, his conception of justice is derived from this hypothetical contract. However, it is curious to think that the author first conceived his principles of justice and then the contract. Therefore, this is an argumentative tool that the author uses to demonstrate how intuitive his theory is (not least because he argues that the two arguments are convergent[19]). However, as has already been pointed out, the author reserves the possibility of altering some of the elements of the original position in order to derive his principles from it, without, however, altering its most fundamental points, which, it seems, would compromise their very essence.

In short, these were the fundamental points of Egalitarian Liberalism. As already mentioned, we have not tried to summarize all the points of the theory, but only to provide a general overview, within what can influence the conclusions of this work.

[19] KYMLICKA, Will. Contemporary Political Philosophy: An Introduction. 2°Ed. Oxford University Press. NY. 2002. Pp. 67-70.

3. AFFIRMATIVE ACTION IN IDEAL AND NON-IDEAL THEORY.

With this brief introduction to John Rawls' thinking, we move on to a more specific analysis of the subject of this work. Without further ado, and starting from the perspective of Robert Taylor[20] , it is understood that, for Justice as Fairness, affirmative action is of great relevance. The point is that, in general, these policies fit into the non-ideal theory, which we intend to explain in more detail below. In order to understand this distinction, it should be borne in mind that the ideal theory is not the same as the ideal theory, but that one does not interfere with the other.

In this sense, affirmative action policy, or at least part of it, can be a suitable remedy for the current effects of past discrimination whose effects still reach the present day or, more closely to the real world, of discrimination that still exists, but each in its own time. In fact, this is the position adopted by Thomas Nagel[21] , a mentor and friend of John Rawls.

It is therefore important to reflect on whether the principles of justice implicit in the theory of Justice as Fairness really imply the application of affirmative action policies and, if so, what the best forms and justifications of affirmative action would be from this perspective.

It is worth remembering that, although the Theory of Justice as Fairness is seen as one of the major factors responsible for having even brought up the debate on Affirmative Supports, John Rawls himself wrote very little or almost nothing explicitly on the subject. Only a few more vague passages. The task was then left to his interpreters, by reading and interpreting the author's writings, as well as through conversations they had

[20] TAYLOR, Robert S. *Rawlsian Affirmative Action. In.* Ethics. Chicago University Press. Chicago, IL. 2009.

[21] NAGEL, Thomas. John Rawls and Affirmative Action. In: The Journal of Blacks in Higher Education, n. 39, pp. 82-84, New York, NY. Spring, 2003.

with him to make his position on the subject clearer.

Before going any further, it is important to conceptualize what is meant by the term affirmative action. Again according to Taylor[22] , affirmative action is characterized as

"(...) a class of public policy that aims to achieve equal opportunities, especially in education and employment, for historically oppressed groups. The approach is forward-looking, motivated by the ideal egalitarian policy in a society 'blind' to gender and color."

Here, then, we have an affirmative support approach in the sense of correcting economic and social distortions. The expression "society blind to gender and color" may carry some negative semantic weight, but the idea is much more one of impartiality in the process of obtaining goods and social positions than of insensitivity to questions of gender and color, as it may sound to the unwary. It should be stressed that what is being affirmed here is the search for a society in which skin color and sexual orientation, distinctions which, in Rawls' terms, are morally arbitrary, have no weight in the process of distributing social goods and positions.

Well, just to present another view on the subject, Joao Feres Junior and Luiz Augusto Campos conceptualize affirmative action as "policies, public or private corporate, that aim to promote a certain under-represented social category in some institutional space or function."[23] However, both are very general concepts. In order to give more materiality to the subject, we take as a reference, based on Robert Taylor[24] , Thomas Nagel's stratified concept of affirmative support. For this author, affirmative support can be grouped into

---

[22] TAYLOR, Robert S. *Rawlsian Affirmative Action. In.* Ethics. Chicago University Press. Chicago, IL. 2009. P. 478. free translation.

[23] JUNIOR, Joao Feres & CAMPOS, Luiz Augusto. *Egalitarian Liberalism and Affirmative Action: from moral theory to public policy. In.* Revista de Sociologia e Politica. v. 21, n. 48, pp. 85-99. Curitiba, PR. December 2013. P. 86.

[24] TAYLOR, Robert S. *Rawlsian Affirmative Action. In.* Ethics. Chicago University Press. Chicago, IL. 2009. P. 478.

five categories, grouped in increasing order of aggressiveness.

Well then, the first category of affirmative action deals with a specific facet of equal opportunities, namely the formal one. Therefore, by guaranteeing this first level of public policy, careers are open to all, with no arbitrary discrimination. This first level draws from the source of the first generation of fundamental rights, where the main concern was equality before the law. Although the perspective is different here, the idea would be exactly "equality before positions".

Nagel calls the second level aggressive formal equality of opportunity. With this, he seeks a self-conscious impartiality that results from training the population, external monitoring and (coercive) legal reinforcement. The idea here is to fight prejudice inside people's heads, performing a function that the literature conceptualizes as preference alteration .[25]

This mechanism can be one of the results of state action, which leads people not to change their behavior, but to change their thinking, or, from another perspective, a qualified change of behavior. In a metaphor for Kantian duty-based action, it's about getting people to change their behavior not because of any sanction effect, but because they believe it's the best course of action.

The third category of affirmative action is concerned with "compensatory aid", i.e. special training and capacity-building programs for less well-off social strata and historically and/or currently discriminated groups. In fact, Brazil has some good examples of this type of affirmative action, such as the recent "Hora do Enem", a free online pre-vestibular course; as well as the classic Telecurso 2000, qualifying young people and adults for the job

[25] On the subject, Cass Sunstein confronts the arguments and concludes that the State is legitimate to act by altering the preferences of individuals, as long as certain requirements are met. See SUNSTEIN, Cass. Legal Interference with Private Preferences. *In.* The University of Chicago Law Review, volume 53, n° 4, Fall, 1986.

market, and the vast TV Escola program.

Moving on to the next category, we come to "soft quotas", i.e. some form of compensatory discrimination in the selection process, notably some level of "starting bonus" for certain groups. This was, in fact, the affirmative action system adopted by the Federal University of Minas Gerais until recently for the entrance exams. At the time, students from public schools received a 10% increase in their marks and those who, in addition to having attended public schools, declared themselves to be black, brown or indigenous received, instead of 10, a 15% increase.

The last category of affirmative action is what Nagel calls "heavy quotas", which require a proportional representation of the beneficiaries of the public policy in the outcome of the processes of division of social goods and positions. In other words, the heavy quota requires the reservation of places for its beneficiaries. Again in the Brazilian context, this is the case of Law No. 12.711/2012, which, in its 1st article, states:

Art. 1° Federal institutions of higher education linked to the Ministry of Education will reserve, in each selection procedure for admission to undergraduate courses, by course and shift, at least 50% (fifty percent) of their places for students who have fully attended secondary school in public schools. Paragraph one. When filling the places referred to in the heading of this article, 50% (fifty percent) must be reserved for students from families with an income equal to or less than 1.5 minimum wages (one and a half minimum wages) per capita.

Art. 2° (VETOED).

Art. 3° In each federal institution of higher education, the vacancies referred to in art. 1° of this Law shall be filled, by course and shift, by self-declared black, brown and indigenous people, in a proportion at least equal to that of black, brown and indigenous people in the population of the unit of the Federation where the institution is located, according to the last census of the Brazilian

Institute of Geography and Statistics (IBGE).

We can see how the law is concerned with reserving 50% of places at Federal Higher Education Institutes for students who attended public schools. In addition, the sole paragraph of the same article and the third article set out ways of dividing up this 50%, taking into account the family's income and declared "rapa".

As an addendum, therefore, the vetoed article 2 of the aforementioned law even included a differentiated selection process for quota holders, which follows below, accompanied by the reasons for the veto:

"Art. 2º Public universities shall select students from secondary education in public schools on the basis of the Performance Coefficient (CR), obtained by means of the arithmetic average of the grades or marks obtained during the period, taking into account the common curriculum to be established by the Ministry of Education.

Single paragraph. Private higher education institutions may adopt the procedure described in the heading of this article in their entrance exams."

Reasons for veto

"The Coefficient of Performance, formed from the grades awarded throughout high school, is not an adequate criterion for evaluating students, since it is not based on a standardized exam common to all candidates and does not follow uniform parameters for assigning grades."

Well, it seems clear that the aim of categories 1 and 2 is notably to eliminate society's prejudices, especially the second one. From the point of view of 3, the perspective seems to be a little more one of seeking out and promoting compensatory public policies in order to level the playing field and improve everyone's position in the search for their place in the sun. Category 4, in turn, interferes with the selection process and, finally, category 5 interferes with the result.

According to Taylor, Justice as Fairness only allows affirmative support up to level 3, and only in the case of non-ideal conditions[26] . At the same time, he presents a single exception for applying category 4 without hurting what he calls the essence of equal opportunities, which he explains later. As a rule, Justice as Fairness would not allow quotas to be "light" or "heavy", even under non-ideal conditions.

Much has already been said about ideal conditions, but it's worth taking a closer look at what exactly is meant by ideal theory. According to John Rawls' ideal theory, the basic structure of society respects three fundamental principles of justice, which are in lexical order of priority. As described above, this priority means that there is a strong hierarchy between the principles and that it cannot be overcome (the priority is of the lexicon, the meaning, the concept of each principle).

For the ideal theory, therefore, there is no point in weighing up the principles of justice, because already in the abstract they each have a different weight: the weighting has already been done in the abstract. The lexical order of the principles mentioned, as discussed in the previous chapter, is as follows:

1. Equal basic freedoms;
2. Equal opportunities;
3. Differences.

However, this alone does not make the theory ideal. Combined with the lexical priority of the principles described above are the ideal conditions, strict observance of established rules (i.e. the absence of relevant injustices within society) and the absence of historical contingencies (e.g. a

[26] TAYLOR, Robert S. *Rawlsian Affirmative Action. In.* Ethics. Chicago University Press. Chicago, IL. 2009. P. 479.

world war).

Given this scenario, and remembering that the lexical order does not allow for exceptions here, equal opportunities cannot be compromised by the principle of difference or even any other principle that is not one of those listed above, for example, efficiency.

With regard to equal opportunities, it should also be noted that it has two facets, also in a lexical series of priority. The first, formal, translates into careers open to talent. This means that everyone who applies for a job has a full chance of getting it without having to face any kind of arbitrary discrimination .[27]

In turn, the other facet, which is substantial, has the maxim of guaranteeing all citizens the chance to compete for jobs and positions, regardless of their circumstances and contingencies. The concern of equity as a state objective in this sense is to avoid unjustified accumulation and concentration of wealth, as well as providing equal educational opportunities .[28]

Having glimpsed the spectrum of ideal theory, which of the categories of Nagelian affirmative support would be morally acceptable?

According to Taylor, only the first, because it is almost confused with the concept of formal equal opportunities. Category 2 contradicts the strict observance of the law and is therefore possible under non-ideal conditions, as we will demonstrate below. On the other hand, it would be acceptable in non-ideal conditions, with social stability as its guiding principle, provided that the

[27] It's worth mentioning that there are distinctions which, even if all the requirements of the ideal theory are met, survive, and that's how it should be. An ideal world does not treat unequals equally, as Aristotle said. The question is the justification behind the distinction. For example, allowing only black actors to play the role of Martin Luther King Jr. and only white actors to play the role of James Earl Ray, his executioner, is a non-arbitrary and morally acceptable form of discrimination.

[28] TAYLOR, Robert S. *Rawlsian Affirmative Action. In.* Ethics. Chicago University Press. Chicago, IL. 2009. P. 480.

ideal has recently been achieved (the possibility of having a voice, albeit a hoarse one, for prejudices from earlier times) and/or if there is a strong context of immigration, which can, as it has in our world, generate strong social tensions and even hatred between equal human beings.

To be clear, the following categories all violate formal equal opportunity, notably the idea advocated by Taylor that it infuses a society blind to gender and skin color. They would therefore not be accepted under these conditions, according to the position described in this text.

This is not about social quotas, which are perhaps the most important in contemporary Brazil. Its discussion is more relevant to non-ideal theory, since, in ideal conditions, respecting the fundamental principles of justice, the adoption of a criterion that increases the social goods that a certain group receives undermines the merit of those in superior positions, providing the latter with less than they are entitled to and the former with more.

As Rawls would say, under ideal conditions, preferential treatment is not compatible with fair equality of opportunity. Taylor raises a further question: if skin color and gender are qualitatively the same as differences in family income and social class[29] ? The question actually reveals a tension between formal and substantial equal opportunities, since skin color and gender are understood to be related to the former, while social class and family income are related to the latter. The justification for this distinction is that one can imagine a world that does not suffer from the evils of sexism and racism, while family and income will always be a problem.

For Justice as Fairness, the tension between formal and substantial equal opportunities exists in non-ideal conditions, where in fact there are still remnants of racism and sexism, however, in view of the strict observance of ideal conditions, this tension disappears in ideal conditions:

[29] TAYLOR, Robert S. *Rawlsian Affirmative Action. In.* Ethics. Chicago University Press. Chicago, IL. 2009. Pp. 482-483.

discrimination there is only
idiosyncratic and absolutely unsystematic, for example, against fans of a certain TV series.

Returning to Rawls' second principle, as already explained, it is made up of two independent principles. The first, with the increase in everyone's advantage in mind, is based on efficiency and difference, so that in ideal conditions, efficiency takes precedence over difference, which is not always justified in non-ideal conditions, because in these, justice takes precedence over efficiency. The second part of the principle has to do with open careers, and therefore with both the formal and substantial aspects of fair equality of opportunity. For the ideal theory, the formal perspective takes precedence over the substantial one, which also falls apart in the non-ideal world for the same reason.

Well then, for Rawls, the different equal opportunities take place at different stages in his sequence of four stages[30] . It is also emphasized that the distinction between the stage at which a certain matter is found depends largely on the need to reach a consensus on it, given the plurality of society. The formal stage is found in the second, in which the constitutional essence is defined; the substantial stage, in the third, is the problem of legislation, which applies the constitutionally defined principles. Basic freedoms, the existential minimum and formal equal opportunities are considered constitutional essences for the theory, each related to one of the fundamental principles of justice.

Rawls believes that formal equality of opportunity is even the basis of self-respect. It is emphasized that even a just society is marked by differences (morally permissible, of course), so that they can, at some level, undermine the basis of the self-respect of those in an inferior position. On the

[30] TAYLOR, Robert S. *Rawlsian Affirmative Action. In.* Ethics. Chicago University Press. Chicago, IL. 2009. P. 484.

other hand, equality of status (formal equal opportunities), as a dimension of political citizenship, also aims to guarantee individual autonomy (the Kantian maxim of treating human beings as ends and not as means). This dimension of equal opportunities also plays an important role in relation to social citizenship, since skin color and gender also affect the careers and social positions occupied.

Thus, under ideal conditions, the formal aspect of equality equitable opportunities overrides the substantial one. In the words of Taylor :[31]

"The elimination of all forms of hierarchy of public status is a sign of having achieved the liberalism that

promises an end to the degradation of both masters and servants."

In non-ideal conditions, the situation is somewhat different, because instead of strict observance and overcoming historical contingencies, there is partial observance of norms and certain contingencies remain. Under these conditions, the lexical priorities of the principle of equal freedom and equal opportunities become fluid .[32]

Therefore, the general concept of justice applies, of which the concept presented in the ideal theory is a type. According to Rawls, as presented above, the general conception of justice makes it possible for the division of social goods to be unequal, as long as the inequality works to the benefit of all, especially the least advantaged. This means that, under this argument, a certain exchange of primary social goods is possible.

Just as in the case of the ideal theory, sexism and racism would obviously be greatly reduced, given the partial observance of the rules, once the differences of degree are respected. It should also be emphasized that

[31] TAYLOR, Robert S. *Rawlsian Affirmative Action. In.* Ethics. Chicago University Press. Chicago, IL. 2009. P. 485. free translation.

[32] Ibid.

Justice as Fairness must seek legitimate ways to guarantee equality for women, blacks and other minorities. Morally arbitrary discrimination leads to socio-economic distortions, which not only reaffirm oppressive stereotypes, but also prevent the participation of those discriminated against as equals. Well, would this protection mean the application of some more aggressive category of affirmative action?

To reiterate, current discrimination and even the lingering effects of past violations do not conform to strict observance, which is one of the reasons why we are now in the non-ideal theory. Well then, maintaining the lexical priority between formal equal opportunities and substantial equal opportunities, in this context, prevents current disadvantages from being eradicated, blocking access to ideal conditions.

Furthermore, a strong affirmative action policy in the first category does indeed solve the problem of present inequalities, but it has little power to resolve the legacy of previous ones. The ideal of equal opportunities will be achieved through policies that strongly attack this legacy, which seems, at first, to go against equal opportunities itself.

In order to delve a little deeper into John Rawls' non-ideal theory, Robert Taylor[33] , drawing on Christine Korsgaard's source, offers a very pedagogical approach. First of all, it's worth mentioning that the great thing to take into account about non-ideal theory is its objective, i.e. achieving ideal conditions. In other words, the goal is a world whose characteristics allow the ideal theory to be applied.

To this end, the deletion of lexical priorities is always allowed on a temporary basis (until the ideal conditions are reached) and instrumentally (in order to achieve them). Therefore, even the strongest forms of affirmative

[33] TAYLOR, Robert S. *Rawlsian Affirmative Action. In.* Ethics. Chicago University Press. Chicago, IL. 2009. Pp. 487-488.

action are allowed (provided the above requirements are met), until the goal is achieved, at which point they must be eliminated again.

Therefore, all affirmative action in non-ideal conditions should aim to make the reality in which it exists a little closer to the one in which the ideal theory can be applied through the necessary means. This mantra, in fact, is a good legitimacy filter for affirmative action, as it is for public policies in general.

From everything we've seen so far, the non-ideal theory would be a good example of a consequentialist theory, since its goal is to achieve another state, and it doesn't even have internal parameters for controlling the means of achieving that goal. This would create a rather disturbing concern within Justice as Fairness, namely, how could a deontological ideal theory with a strong Kantian tinge make use of a non-ideal consequentialist theory in order to be achieved?

As Korsgaard points out, according to Taylor, ideal theory is also, in a way, a guide to choices among non-ideal alternatives. In other words, the lights of ideal theory not only guide the paths within its domains, but even illuminate fields that are not yet ideal. In this context, as well as being effective in achieving his goal, Taylor[34] outlines at least three important parameters of choice that should be taken into account in non-ideal deliberation.

The first of these insists that the non-ideal theory must be consistent with its general conception of justice, which has already been demonstrated. Secondly, the non-ideal theory must mirror the lexical priority of the ideal theory in choosing the order of its axes. In other words, although the strict lexical series of principles no longer prevails here, the axes relating to the various principles must be ordered according to their lexical series under ideal conditions.

[34] TAYLOR, Robert S. *Rawlsian Affirmative Action. In.* Ethics. Chicago University Press. Chicago, IL. 2009. P. 489-490.

Last but not least, the ideal theory must be consistent with the essence of the ideal theory. The latter, in fact, does not have to follow the letter of the principles, but must act in accordance with the purpose, the essence of each of them. Of course, it is not easy to identify what the essence of the principle is and the restrictions that derive from it, which must be done on a case-by-case basis. However, ignoring these restrictions can lead to policies that are definitively irreconcilable with the dense moral principles developed in ideal theory.

Returning to the question that has been formulated and is still open, let's start with category 3 of affirmative action. Well, the central point of equal opportunities is to enhance the natural abilities and ambitions of citizens, so that they are able to compete effectively for jobs and positions in the basic structure of a social sphere in which the same abilities and ambitions can be better developed and exercised, enabling individuals to achieve self-fulfilment.

However, the scenario described above only exists if social contingencies (family, class, gender, skin color...) are effectively neutralized. This is the purpose of category 3 affirmative action, which is perfectly in line with the essence of fair equality of opportunity, although it technically contradicts the strict letter of the same principle, since it is not blind to gender or skin color .[35]

It is interesting to note that the policies in this third category do not directly interfere with the outcome or the rules of the game, i.e. the process of obtaining goods and social positions. Their target is all forms of preparation. In Taylor's very felicitous metaphor, this kind of affirmative action takes the weights off the legs of certain participants in the race .[36]

---

[35] TAYLOR, Robert S. *Rawlsian Affirmative Action. In.* Ethics. Chicago University Press. Chicago, IL. 2009. P. 491.

[36] TAYLOR, Robert S. *Rawlsian Affirmative Action. In.* Ethics. Chicago University Press. Chicago, IL. 2009. P. 492.

Furthermore, this form of affirmative action is also compatible with Pure Procedural Justice[37] , according to which there is no independent criterion for the correct outcome. Rawls argues that his thoughts on the basic structure of society and on fair equality of opportunity lead to the idea of treating distributive shares as a problem of pure procedural justice. According to him, this deals with the intuitive notion of "designing the social system so that the outcome is fair, whatever it is, at least as long as it is within certain limits."[38]

According to Rawls, pure procedural justice is best understood by comparing perfect and imperfect procedural justice. For the latter, there is "an independent criterion for defining what is fair division"[39] , defined independently, separately from the procedure and to which the latter must adhere. Furthermore, it is characterized by the fact that, although there are independent parameters for defining the appropriate result, there is no feasible procedure that will infallibly produce that fair result, which is why it is treated as imperfect. For the author, the criminal process is an example of this, since the desired result is that the defendant is found guilty, only and only if he has in fact committed the allegations imputed to him .[40]

Perfect (or pure) procedural justice, on the other hand, has no such criterion outside the procedure, but only the fair procedure itself as a parameter. It is from this, therefore, that the equally correct or fair result is drawn, regardless of what it is, as long as the procedure has been correctly followed. Finally, this conception of justice assumes that the just procedure has the power to transcribe its justice to its result only if it is followed.

Thus, category 3 affirmative support associated with a procedure that is blind to color and gender (as well as being fair in its other possibilities)

---

[37] TAYLOR, Robert S. *Rawlsian Affirmative Action. In.* Ethics. Chicago University Press. Chicago, IL. 2009. Pp. 493.
[38] RAWLS, John. A Theory of Justice. Martins Fontes. Sao Paulo, SP. 2008. P. 103.
[39] Ibid.
[40] RAWLS, John. A Theory of Justice. Martins Fontes. Sao Paulo, SP. 2008. P. 104.

produces a fair result. Any subsequent interference with this result would mean tainting a result that already has the stamp of correctness and fairness on it. That's why the bonus or reservation of places would taint the results of this procedure and would therefore not be accepted even in situations that are not ideal for John Rawls' theory.

A fair distribution is therefore one that emerges from a fair procedure, i.e. one that neutralizes social contingencies through affirmative support of the third kind at the entrance and formal equal opportunities (affirmative action of the first kind) in the process. If this is indeed true, then the latest forms of affirmative action, light and heavy quotas, violate the essence of equal opportunities.

It seems that it only makes sense to accept the light and heavy quotas insofar as they compensate for what the others have failed to do. Taylor[41] points out that Thomas Nagel's position, for example, is that categories 4 and 5 of affirmative action are necessary in the face of unfair disadvantages not overcome by training or special preparatory programs. In these cases, then, either the effects of discrimination are accepted or a system of compensatory discrimination is created, by means of "light" and/or "heavy" quotas.

Taylor[42] also presents a final problem for the application of category 4 and 5 affirmative policies. A flaw in their application which closes the argument described above. Well, the problem with applying the fourth and fifth categories of affirmative support to compensate for the result is that we don't know what the result of a genuinely pure competition will be. This reinforces the maxim of pure procedural justice, which does not provide criteria for evaluating the results, but only means of making the procedure fair, from which the results are presumed to be (absolutely) fair.

---

[41] Ibid.

[42] TAYLOR, Robert S. *Rawlsian Affirmative Action. In.* Ethics. Chicago University Press. Chicago, IL. 2009. P. 494.

This is not a problem of effectiveness (of the procedures), but of the very epistemology of the concept. In other words, the pure procedural nature of equal opportunities, since it doesn't provide a criterion for evaluating the results, means that judging has to be suspended until the fair procedure has been achieved. At this point, however, such a criterion would already be useless, as would category 4 and 5 affirmative support, because the result is already fair in pure procedural terms.

What's more, it's worth noting how arranging pure procedural results under the argument of justice is one of those slippery slope arguments[43] , giving the impression of great malleability, easily corrupted by those in power. In other words, changing the outcome after the fair procedure sounds arbitrary and contrary to the essence of equal opportunities, as long as one accepts that this translates as an application of pure procedural justice to the domain of the distribution of jobs and positions, as Rawls clearly does.

However, there is also criticism of the *quantum* implied by the application of quotas. In the case of "light", what is the right percentage value to reflect the essence of equal opportunities in order to justify a result that is not? The question, in simpler terms, is: what percentage increase should a candidate receive in order to correct current discrimination and the effects of previous discrimination they face? In the case of "heavy" quotas, the question becomes a little more complicated, but in the end, the problem of *quantum* is also latent here. In this sense, what percentage of places would Justice as Fairness advocate as fair and due for those who have faced arbitrary

[43] The slippery slope argument or continuum fallacy is based on
in general terms, to assume that the intermediate stages between two points are indifferent, or rather that it makes no difference which stage you are at within the continuum between two points. The analogy here is that the idea of the absence of an independent criterion can be used by those in power to "broaden the state of justice" by increasing the number of situations it covers. In other words, what is feared here is that, because there is no final criterion, the argument that certain states are fair because they have respected the procedures is used ideologically, without always taking care to make people reflect on whether the fair procedure has really been respected. For further clarification on this type of argument, we strongly recommend strongly: http://aquitemfilosofiasim.blogspot.com.br/2012/11/formas-de-argumento-ladeira-slippery_4276.html

discrimination in some way?

Perhaps the latter is exactly the major issue raised by opponents of affirmative action policies in Brazil today. The law that established the current model was quite revolutionary and aggressive in this sense, as it guarantees 50% of places in public higher education institutions to its beneficiaries. Much has been said about this figure being too high.

The point is that this amount is for social quotas (students who attended high school entirely in public schools, according to the first article of the law). Within this amount, the law further subdivides it, safeguarding racial quotas and quotas for low-income families. However, we will take a closer look at this issue in the next chapter.

To close the subject, by saying the above, we do not mean that Justice as Fairness is not interested in abolishing racial or sexual prejudice or arbitrary discrimination of any kind. Quite the opposite, in fact. A well-ordered society does not tolerate this kind of attitude, having been built to exterminate it. What was discussed here was the adoption of affirmative action, in view of Rawls' ideal and non-ideal theory, as has already been exhaustively mentioned.

This was the overview we wanted to draw up on the subject. As already mentioned, this is not a final answer, but just a way forward for discussion. In view of the above, there is still a concern to relate what has been described here to the policy of compensatory discrimination adopted in Brazil. This is the task of the next chapter.

4. THE QUESTION OF SOCIAL QUOTAS.

As already mentioned in this text, we have finally reached the point that is most relevant to the Brazilian context: social quotas. Social quotas are aimed at the poorest sections of society and in Brazil are basically based on two criteria: income or attendance at public schools.

By taking income as the standard for an aggressive type of public policy, such as category 5 affirmative action, it becomes clear that the result of the current process of distributing goods and positions goes against intuitive standards of justice. In this sense, it is not difficult to see that Brazil is not the best place in the world for the less fortunate, much less that the design of the social pyramid has been structurally changed.

The indices of social inequality here, therefore, are profound and growing .[44]

There is also an unacceptable disparity between public and private primary education. Brazil's history shows that the government's interest since the time of independence has been to invest in higher education, leaving the stages of education that come before it in the background. So much so that federal universities are always hotly contested and have, even with all their problems, a much higher quality of education than the average private university.

Taking into account that there is an entrance exam for higher education, it is quite obvious that the picture described above creates an uncomfortable distortion. Those who can afford quality private primary education do so, preparing themselves in a much more qualified way. Meanwhile, the lower-income population, who can't afford it, go to public

[44] On this subject, from a global perspective, see Thomas Piketty, "Capital in the 21st Century". For data from Brazil, under the guidance of Piketty himself, see Marc Morgan Mila, "Income Concentration in a Context of Late Development: An Investigation of Top Incomes in Brazil using Tax Records, 1933-2013". Available at: http://piketty.pse.ens.fr/files/MorganMila2015.pdf.

schools, which don't always receive the investment they need for a decent education. The competition in the old entrance exam, now ENEM, is thus compromised from the point of view of social justice.

Without an inclusive policy of this kind, the population that can afford private education would end up (and, for a long time, did end up) occupying the majority of places in public universities, with an even greater predominance in the most competitive courses such as Law, Engineering and Medicine. In other words, unfair preparation leads to unfair competition, which ends up closing the doors of public higher education to those who need it most.

From this situation, apart from the question of injustice towards the poorest, we can conclude that this is an inefficient and unfair allocation of public spending. This is because a large amount of money is invested in public higher education so that it can be enjoyed by the wealthiest class of the population, who can afford higher education. As a result, intellectual disparity is increasing and the intellectual exclusion of those at the bottom of the social scale .[45]

Given this scenario, it is clear that Brazil, and it hurts to say this, is not even close to the non-ideal conditions envisioned by John Rawls. Firstly, there is no way of imagining that Brazilian society is in partial compliance with the rules in the face of its overcrowded judiciary, symbolized by a supreme court that hears more than 100,000 cases a year[46] . Added to this is the strong class distinction and prejudice that the less well-off suffer, creating strong social tensions and not systematically erasing arbitrary discrimination.

The combination of these factors means that the rejection of more

[45] In this sense, see the discussion on bacharelismo, for example, in Sergio Adorno, "Os aprendizes do poder. Liberal bacharelismo in Brazilian politics".
[46] By way of example, http://www.valor.com.br/legislacao/4048192/numero-de- processo-em-tramitacao-e-assustador-diz-ministra-do-stf, accessed on July 13, 2016.

aggressive affirmative support made in the second chapter does not apply to the current Brazilian context. It is understood that the most aggressive affirmative policies in Brazil today genuinely meet the requirements of the second principle of justice, notably its aspect of equal opportunities.

This synthesizes the two approaches of the second Ralwsean principle of justice in its final statement :[47]

"Social and economic inequalities must be arranged in such a way that they both (a) provide the maximum benefit for the least advantaged and (b) are linked to jobs and positions open to all under conditions of equal opportunity."

This definitive formulation presents two principles of justice, as already mentioned. In this sense, social differences have to work (a) towards the betterment of those in the worst social positions and (b) in a context of making jobs and social positions available to everyone on a fairly equal basis.

In this sense, the issue is to seek, through social quotas, to promote material equality between candidates from public and private schools when competing for a place at a public university. Of course, from the point of view of Justice as Fairness, the best thing would be to provide a quality public education system, which enables students' cognitive activities to develop properly and brings them as close as possible to full parity of arms with those from private schools.

On the other hand, given Brazil's reality, achieving this goal is a dream too far away for the current generation. In this sense, justice is uncomfortable with the idea of maintaining the exclusion of millions simply because of the lack of current organization. Education is a basic social right of all and a duty of the state, under the terms of the caput of art. 6 and art. 255 of

[47] RAWLS, John. A theory of justice. Martins Fontes. Sao Paulo. 2006. P. 100.

the 1988 Constitution[48] . This being the case, implementing affirmative action in categories 4 and 5 with a social bias is a quicker solution to the problem, with a view to improving the conditions of those who occupy the lower rungs of the social ladder.

In fact, it seems possible to draw an analogy here with the requirements already mentioned in this text. To do this, we take the notes on affirmative action in non-ideal theory, discussed in the previous chapter and based on Robert Taylor[49] . In this sense, with the necessary caveats, the criteria that limit and guide public policies in the transition from non-ideal to ideal conditions could be applied to the transition from real (Brazilian) conditions to non-ideal ones. In this way, the implementation of category 4 and 5 affirmative action must necessarily be marked by transience (because it is a palliative that the non-ideal theory, as demonstrated, does not support) and be instrumentally justified in order to achieve non-ideal conditions.

Such policies also need to be consistent with the general concept of justice, mirror the lexical order of the principles and respect their essence. This seems to be the case, since these programs work to reduce social inequalities in Brazil by increasing access to free higher education. Added to this is the idea that, under real conditions, there may even be greater weight given to the principle of difference, further improving the situation of the poorest, since the need for justice is reinforced in this context.

In fact, as has already been shown, Robert Taylor believes that the affirmative actions of categories 4 and 5 are not compatible with John Rawls' theory. However, he himself accepted that, when faced with interventions from

---

[48] Art. 6: Social rights are education, health, food, work, housing, transportation, leisure, security, social security, maternity and childhood protection, and assistance to the destitute, in the form of this Constitution.
Art. 205. Education, the right of all and the duty of the State and the family, shall be promoted and encouraged with the collaboration of society, with a view to the full development of the person, their preparation for the exercise of citizenship and their qualification for work.

[49] TAYLOR, Robert S. *Rawlsian Affirmative Action. In.* Ethics. Chicago University Press. Chicago, IL. 2009. Pp. 491-494.

categories 1 to 3 that have not been effective, it would be morally acceptable to use 4 or 5, provided that this was done in order to make the previous policies more effective[50] . He emphasizes that the use of these categories should be kept to a minimum, so that they would only be allowed as temporary enablers of the previous categories. It seems that this is the background to the Brazilian situation, since it is understood that only the use of affirmative action categories 1 to 3 would not be effective enough, thus not dispensing with the more aggressive categories to make them viable.

As already touched on at one point in the text, the problem of the *number of* places reserved for students from public schools is an epistemological question of the so-called "heavy" quotas. However, given the data on Brazilian social inequality, it is understood that this would not be an obstacle to the implementation of this policy and that, however dubious, unscientific and based mainly on a mere intuition of justice, the value implemented by the current Brazilian legislation does not seem unreasonable.

Regarding the issue of racial quotas in Brazil, this is a very complex problem, not least because racism here tends to manifest itself less explicitly, often making it difficult to perceive. This makes racial prejudice not only odious, but also hypocritical. For affirmative action up to category 3, as shown above, Justice as Fairness provides good justification. We now turn to the use of affirmative action in categories 4 and 5.

We don't intend to invest too much in the subject, but it shouldn't go unanswered. Thus, we have to take into account the extent to which racial prejudice, beyond social issues, harms the distribution of goods and social positions in real Brazilian society. In the case of a problem that undermines the justice of equitable equality of opportunities or create privileges (and not differences that improve the well-being of all), must also be combated, even by

---

[50] TAYLOR, Robert S. *Rawlsian Affirmative Action. In.* Ethics. Chicago University Press. Chicago, IL. 2009. Pp. 501-502.

categories 4 and 5 of affirmative action.

As a result, the essence of Rawlse's theory of justice justifies the use of social criteria such as income and attendance at public schools to reduce social inequalities, making it possible to compete more fairly for jobs and social positions. In this sense, the principles of fair equality of opportunity and difference are safeguarded, since such policies enable fairer competition from the point of view of the socially worse-off classes.

5. CONCLUSION.

John Rawls' vision has profoundly revolutionized Western political philosophy, since it has revived its debate. In addition, a series of fundamental concepts for the current paradigm of the Democratic Rule of Law derive from the American author's work, such as the existential minimum and affirmative action, the subject of this work. In fact, such is the author's influence on Brazilian law that he was even quoted by Justice Ricardo Lewandowski in his report on the Arguigao de Descumprimento de Preceito Fundamental 186, which questioned the constitutionality of Brazilian affirmative action .[51]

As already pointed out, it is curious that the author has said little or nothing about the subject. Apparently, he only expressly addresses the issue, albeit somewhat inconclusively, in the following passage from his book "Justice as Fairness: A Reaffirmation"[52] , in free translation:

"It has been seen that the two principles of justice apply to citizens identified by their levels of primary social goods. It is natural to ask: why are race and gender distinctions not explicitly included among the three contingencies noted above (§16)? How can anyone ignore historical facts such as slavery (in the US South before the War of Secession) and inequalities between men and women resulting from the absence of measures to make the extra-female burden of bearing, raising and educating children a social good, as well as to ensure their equal opportunities?
The answer is that it is mainly concerned with the ideal theory: the narrative of the well-ordered society of justice as equity."

---

[51] BRAZIL. *Arguigao de descumprimento de preceito fundamental 186, STF.* http://redir.stf.ius.br/paginadorpub/paginador.isp?docTP=TP&docID=6984693. Rapporteur Minister Ricardo Lewandowski. 2012. Accessed on July 12, 2016. P. 7.

[52] RAWLS, J. & KELLY, E. *Justice as Fairness: A restatement.* Harvard University Press. Cambridge, MA. 2001. Pp. 64-65.

On the other hand, affirmative action is much debated among Rawls' interpreters[53] . This is the context of this work, which sought to present general notions of egalitarian liberalism, apply a stratified concept of affirmative action to the theory and present a solution for Brazilian social quotas.

Bearing in mind the notion presented and the concepts of ideal and non-ideal theory, the result found, based on Robert Taylor's work, was surprising to say the least. It is understood that the theory does not provide a basis for any and all types of quota, and that, in fact, the concept would be restrictive. This does not mean that Justice as Fairness is a sexist, racist or even oppressive theory of minorities. The idea is that, as conditions get closer to the ideal, the increased observance of the rules and the reduction of morally arbitrary social inequalities mean that those forms of discrimination are overcome. For this reason, policies that support minorities would be overcompensating, since the majority of prejudices have already been overcome. Nor would social quotas have any place here, since, as society evolves, the social positions that individuals occupy are increasingly theirs.

On the other hand, the distance from these conditions makes it possible for gender and color discrimination to reverberate in less than ideal conditions and open up space for programs that promote special preparation for oppressed groups. An even greater distance from these conditions would even allow for a policy of increasing the grades obtained in the selection process or even reserving places in the final result.

The latter position, although more controversial, seems to demand justice when the context is too far removed from the conditions envisioned by Rawls. In this sense, taking the Brazilian reality as an example, the bold quota policy adopted by Law 12.711/2012, which reserves 50% of public higher

[53] NAGEL, Thomas. John Rawls and Affirmative Action. In: The Journal of Blacks in Higher Education, n. 39, pp. 82-84, New York, NY. Spring, 2003. P. 83.

education places for students from public schools, seems to be right, given the social inequality in the country. However, throughout the text we have avoided discussing the *quantum of* these quotas precisely because of their incommensurability. The prevailing argument was that such a figure is intuitive and in line with a considered judgment on the subject, since the gap between private and public secondary education in Brazil is evident and abysmal.

Finally, it is hoped that this text has paved the way for a better understanding of Justice as Fairness and one of its practical implications. It is also believed to have provided a good foundation for an inclusive and very healthy public policy, the aims of which are aimed at reducing social inequalities in the country.

6. BIBLIOGRAPHICAL REFERENCES.

ADORNO, Sergio. *The apprentices of power. Liberal bachelorism in Brazilian politics.* Editora Paz e Terra. Rio de Janeiro, RJ. 1988.

BARRY, Brian. *The Liberal Theory of Justice: A Critical Examination of the Principal Doctrines in A Theory of Justice by John Rawls.* Oxford University Press. London, UK. 1973.

BRAZIL. *Arguigao de descumprimento de preceito fundamental 186, STF.* Rapporteur Minister Ricardo Lewandowski. 2012. Available at: <http://www.stf.jus.br/arquivo/cms/noticiaNoticiaStfArquivo/anexo/ADPF186.pdf>. Accessed on July 12, 2016.

DANIELS, Norman. *Reading Rawls: critical studies on Rawls' a theory of justice.* Stanford University Press. Stanford, CA. 1989.

DWORKIN, Ronald. *A Matter of Principle. Cambridge.* Harvard University Press. Cambridge, MA. 1985.

. *Justice for Hedgehogs.* Harvard University Press. Cambridge, MA. 2011.

. *Sovereign Virtue.* Harvard University Press. Cambridge, MA. 2002.

. *Taking Rights Seriously.* Harvard University Press. Cambridge, MA. 1977.

FREEMAN, Samuel (Org.) *The Cambridge Companion to Rawls.* Cambridge University Press. New York, NY. 2003.

. *Rawls.* Taylor & Francis e-Library. 2007.

FERNANDES, Bernardo Gongalves. *Constitutional Law Course.* 4ª Ed. Editora JusPODIVM. Salvador, BA. 2012.

HART, Hebert L. A. *Rawls on Liberty and its Priority.* University of Chicaco

Law Review. Chicago, IL.1973.

JUNIOR, Joao Feres & CAMPOS, Luiz Augusto. *Egalitarian Liberalism and Affirmative Action: from moral theory to public policy. In.* Revista de Sociologia e Politica. v. 21, n. 48, pp. 85-99. Curitiba, PR. December 2013.

KUKATHAS, Chandran & PETTIT, Philip. *Rawls: A Theory of Justice and its Critics.* Editora Gradiva. Lisbon, PT. 1995.

KYMLICKA, Will. *Contemporary Political Philosophy.* Martins Fontes. Sao Paulo, SP 2006.

MENDES, Gilmar Ferreira; BRANCO, Paulo Gustavo Gonet. *Constitutional Law Course.* 7th Ed. Editora Saraiva. Sao Paulo, SP. 2012.

MILA, Marc M. *Income Concentration in a Context of Late Development: An Investigation of Top Incomes in Brazil using Tax Records, 1933-2013.*

Available at: <http://piketty.pse.ens.fr/files/MorganMila2015.pdf>. Accessed on June 13, 2016.

NAGEL, Thomas. 1973. *Equal Treatment and Compensatory Discrimination. Philosophy and Public Affairs,* v. 2, n. 4, pp. 348-363. Princeton. Summer, 1973.

. *John Rawls and Affirmative Action. In: The Journal of Blacks in Higher Education,* n. 39, pp. 82-84, New York, NY. Spring, 2003.

PERRY, B. A. *The Michigan Affirmative Action Cases, Landmark Law Cases & American Society.* University of Kansas Press. Lawrence, KA. 2007.

PIKETTY, Thomas. *Capital in the 21st Century.* Intrinseca. Rio de Janeiro. 2014.

RAWLS, John. *A Theory of Justice.* 2nd Ed. Harvard University Press.

Cambridge, MA.1999.

. *Lectures on the History of Political Philosophy.* (Org. Samuel Freeman), Harvard University Press. Cambridge, MA. 2007.

. *Political Liberalism (Expanded Edition).* Columbia University Press. New York, NY. 2005.

. *A Theory of Justice.* Martins Fontes. Sao Paulo, SP. 2008.

RAWLS, J. & KELLY, E. *Justice as Fairness: A restatement.* Harvard University Press. Cambridge, MA. 2001.

SUNSTEIN, Cass. *Legal Interference with Private Preferences. In.* The University of Chicago Law Review, volume 53, n° 4, Fall, 1986.

TAYLOR, Robert S. *Rawlsian Affirmative Action. In.* Ethics. Chicago University Press. Chicago, IL. 2009.

MIX
Papier aus verantwortungsvollen Quellen
Paper from responsible sources
FSC® C105338

Printed by Books on Demand GmbH, Norderstedt / Germany